PACKAGE DESIGN

Surface Area and Volume

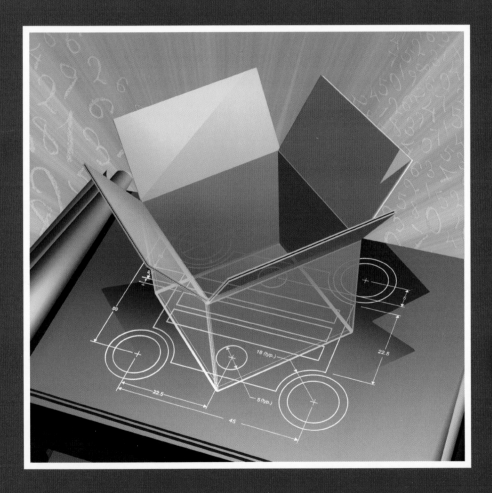

Chloe Lane

Consultants

Pamela Dase, M.A.Ed.
National Board Certified Teacher

Barbara Talley, M.S.
Texas A&M University

Publishing Credits

Dona Herweck Rice, *Editor-in-Chief*
Robin Erickson, *Production Director*
Lee Aucoin, *Creative Director*
Timothy J. Bradley, *Illustration Manager*
Sara Johnson, M.S.Ed., *Senior Editor*
Aubrie Nielsen, M.S.Ed., *Associate Education Editor*
Jennifer Kim, M.A.Ed., *Associate Education Editor*
Neri Garcia, *Senior Designer*
Stephanie Reid, *Photo Editor*
Rachelle Cracchiolo, M.S.Ed., *Publisher*

Image Credits

Teacher Created Materials

5301 Oceanus Drive
Huntington Beach, CA 92649-1030
http://www.tcmpub.com
ISBN 978-1-4333-3460-3
© 2012 Teacher Created Materials, Inc.

TABLE OF CONTENTS

THE BOX CAUGHT MY EYE!

Think about the last time you went to a store to buy something. You might have been looking for food that you have each day, like milk or cereal. Maybe you were buying something special, such as a video game or a new DVD. You might have known exactly what to buy, or maybe you had to look around before deciding what you wanted. How did you make your choice? Did you notice the package that your product came in?

Making Packages Appealing

Packaging plays a big part in **advertising** a product. Advertising is announcing or promoting a product, service, or event. The goal of advertising is to get people to buy or use a product. Companies spend billions of dollars on advertising each year.

Commuters near the busy Shibuya Station in Tokyo have many product advertisements to look at near the train station.

You may not be someone who always pays close attention to the packaging that products come in, but some people do. All different kinds of companies want to make sure that their products are the most interesting on the shelf. When shoppers have a lot of choices, companies want to make sure their products are the ones you reach for and put in your cart. They want the package to catch your eye.

SHAPE AND SIZE MATTER

One important aspect of any product's package is its shape. **Consumers** (kuhn-SOO-merz) expect to see certain items packaged and sold in specific ways. For example, shoppers want new DVDs to come in the same size cases as their other DVDs.

Sometimes a certain package shape is necessary for the product to function well. Making tissue boxes in the shape of a **cube** makes sense because a box can sit on a bathroom counter or a desk. A box of tissue in the shape of a sphere would not be able to function in the same way, so most shoppers would not choose to buy it.

Many products that you shop for come in boxes that are **rectangular prisms**. The **volume** of a rectangular prism is measured in cubic units. Volume determines the number of cubes of a certain size that will fill a **three-dimensional** (dih-MEN-shuhn-uhl) space.

Tissue boxes, books, and DVDs all come in similar-shaped packaging.

Volume is the amount of space occupied by a three-dimensional object.

Look at the cereal box below. Answer the following questions on volume about the box itself—not considering the cereal that might be inside it.

a. How can you find the number of cubes in the layer at the top of the box?

b. How many of these layers are there in the whole box?

c. What is the total number of cubes in the box?

d. Explain why the **formula** for the volume of a rectangular prism is Volume = length × width × height ($V = lwh$).

e. Use the volume formula to find the volume of a box with the dimensions 29.3 cm × 22.7 cm × 5.3 cm. Round your answer to the nearest hundredth.

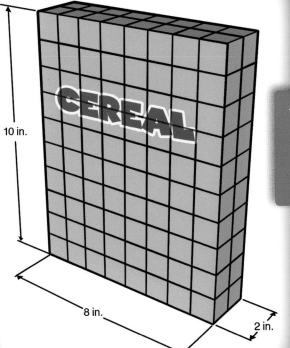

10 in.

8 in.

2 in.

The volume of this box is measured in cubic inches (in.³). It measures how many 1-inch cubes would fill the box.

Size is another **criterion** (krahy-TEER-ee-uhn) for buyers to consider. Many products come in a variety of sizes. For example, it makes sense to buy a small can of tomato sauce instead of a large one if the smaller one holds the exact amount needed for a pizza recipe. Likewise, for a cereal that everyone in a family likes, buying large boxes of it would make more sense than buying small boxes. Larger packages of food last longer and are often more cost effective, too.

Green Packaging

With the amount of waste at an all-time high worldwide, many companies are using more environmentally-friendly packaging. They are very interested in packages made from recyclable materials. By purchasing items packaged with materials that can be recycled, consumers can reduce packaging waste and help the environment.

Have you ever opened a bag of chips or box of raisins and thought the package seemed half empty? The reason for that is because the items settle into their package and do not take up as much space as they did when they were first put in the box. The labeling and pricing for these types of items is usually based on weight, not volume.

LET'S EXPLORE MATH

You are designing boxes for a manufacturer (man-yuh-FAK-cher-er) and you want a packing box with a volume of 40 ft.^{3}. If the base of your box has the dimensions shown, what is the height of the box?

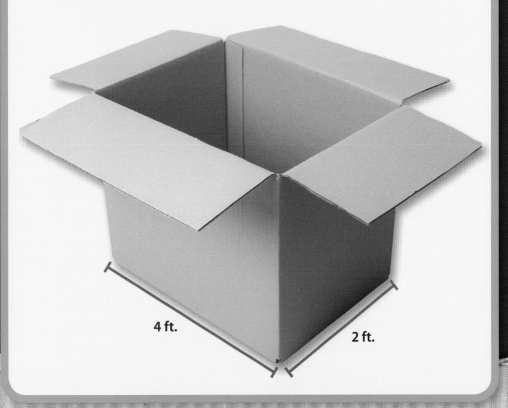

4 ft.

2 ft.

BEAT THE COMPETITION

Companies spend a lot of time thinking about the best possible way to package a product. They have to consider size and shape. They look at how the product will be used, and decide if the packaging is appropriate. They also pay very close attention to their **competitors** (kuhm-PET-i-terz). Since companies want the most desirable product on the market, they have to know what similar products look like that are on the same store shelves.

Think about how soup is packaged. Some companies only sell their soups in a **cylindrical** (si-LIN-dri-kuhl) can. Others prefer to package their soups in a bowl-shaped carton. Still others sell soup as a dry mix in a paper package. The same product that comes in different types of packaging gives consumers a choice about what works best for them.

To find the volume of a cylinder, first find the **area** of the circular base (πr^2, where r represents the **radius**) then multiply by the height (h).
$$V = \pi r^2 h$$
The volume of a cylinder is measured in cubic units just like any other three-dimensional object. When you imagine it filled with cubes, though, some of those cubes will not be whole because of its rounded shape.

$V = \pi(2)^2(5) = 62.8 \text{ in.}^3$

2 in.

5 in.

There is even competition in the world of chocolate! Some chocolate bars are sold in a rectangular shape. Other chocolate makers try to get creative and sell their chocolate products in different shapes. The chocolate may come as a pyramid, a sphere, or a cylinder. Foods of these shapes require creative packaging.

LET'S EXPLORE MATH

Compare the volumes of two different types of soup containers. Use 3.14 for the value of π.

a. Find the volume of Soup A's container.

b. What is the area of Soup B's circular base? Round your answer to the nearest hundredth.

c. What is the volume of Soup B's container? Round your answer to the nearest hundredth.

d. Which soup package has the greater volume?

e. Why is the formula for finding the volume of Soup A different from the formula for finding the volume of Soup B?

MAKING IT FIT

Packaging must always be the right fit for whatever is inside it. But how do you package oddly-shaped products that are not perfect cubes, cylinders, or rectangular prisms? How do companies create packages for pears, for example? One way to help make good decisions about packaging items like these is to take accurate measurements.

Skip the Packaging

Many products come with no packaging at all. They come straight out of their shipping box and get placed right on the shelf. Of course, store owners still have to label them with prices. Some people even argue that food products with no packaging (e.g., fruits, vegetables, meat, and fish) are healthier for you. Skipping the packaging helps reduce waste, too.

One measurement of the size of a package is its **surface area**. The surface area of a solid figure is the total area of all its faces. If you were to unfold the solid, the **two-dimensional** pattern it forms is called a **net**. Finding the area of each face of a net will give you the surface area of the solid. Surface area is measured in **square units**. That means surface area determines the number of squares of a certain size that will cover a surface.

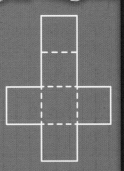

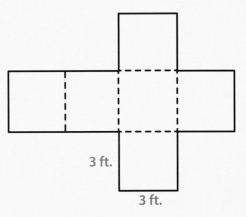

LET'S EXPLORE MATH

Look at this shipping box in the shape of a cube. Find its surface area.

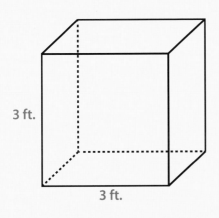

3 ft.

3 ft.

3 ft.

3 ft.

a. How can you find the surface area of this cube?

b. What is the area of one face of the cube?

c. What is the surface area of the cube? Label your answer in square feet (ft.²).

DON'T TOSS THE PACKAGING!

What do you do with packaging when you are finished with it? Some packages are used until the product that is inside is all gone, like an orange juice container or a bottle of hair gel. But other packages are just containers that help you get the product from the store to your home. Then you no longer need them.

When that happens, hopefully you are able to recycle the packaging. This is especially true for packaging made of paper, plastic, and glass. Perhaps you can even "recycle" a package, such as a shoebox or a yogurt container, by using it for another purpose.

Bring Your Own Bag

Many people are now using reusable shopping bags instead of getting a paper or plastic bag at the grocery store. How do you keep from using packaging altogether? Some people work hard to avoid any waste. They make good choices, picking items that come in reusable containers. For example, they might fill glass jars that they already have with **bulk** liquid soaps or shampoo. Shoppers may also use their own containers when buying bulk cereal, pasta, oatmeal, and spices.

Cardboard boxes come in all different sizes. Some are cubes and some are rectangular prisms. Find the surface area of the rectangular prism below.

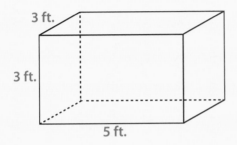

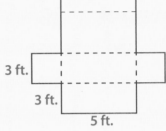

a. What is the total area of the front and back of the box?

b. What is the total area of the two sides of the box?

c. What is the total area of the top and bottom of the box?

d. What is the surface area of the box? Label your answer in square feet (ft.²).

e. Use your work to write a formula for the surface area of a rectangular prism. (*Hint:* Use *l* for length, *w* for width, and *h* for height in your formula.)

Don't reuse or recycle immediately, though! There are good reasons to keep packaging for at least a few days. If you change your mind about a product, you might need the packaging to return or exchange it. Many stores want items returned in the original packages. This is especially true for electronic items, like CDs, DVDs, video games, or cell phones. Keeping an item packaged as it was when you bought it shows that you have not used the product, and allows a store to resell it to another customer.

PACKAGING SAFETY

Some products require special packaging to keep consumers safe. Items like **over-the-counter drugs**, mouthwash, and contact lens solution are sealed with **tamper-resistant** packaging. This packaging helps shoppers know if a product may be **contaminated** by making it obvious if a product has been opened. Types of tamper-resistant packaging include plastic seals, tape, break-away caps, and foil pouches that must be broken to reach the product.

Warning Labels

Some products need to be labeled so that consumers know they are made for older children or adults. Medications often have labels that warn patients about side effects, such as drowsiness. Likewise, other products warn people not to purchase or use them unless they are a certain age. Alcohol, tobacco products, and medicines include age-related warnings.

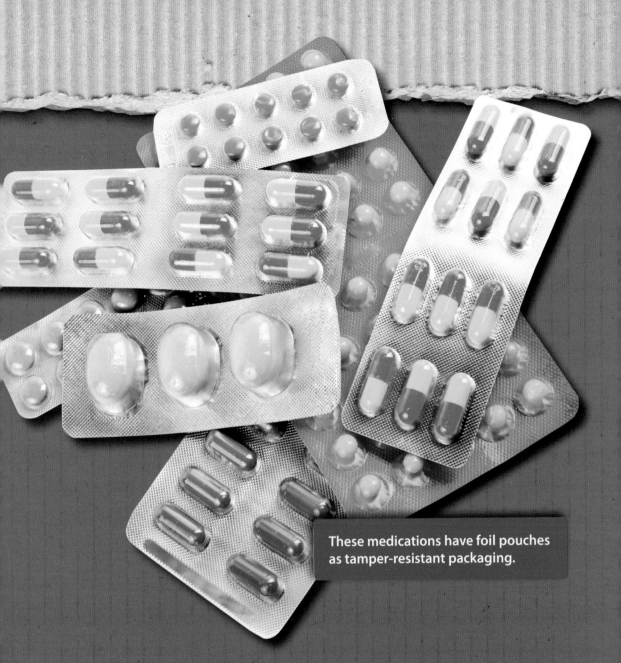

These medications have foil pouches as tamper-resistant packaging.

Child-resistant packaging is required on products that could be dangerous to children. Many of these products come in bottles that use safety caps to keep children from opening them. Prescription drugs, some over-the-counter drugs, and chemicals use safety caps. Sometimes safety packaging can be difficult to open, but it helps to keep consumers safe.

A PACKAGE WITHIN A PACKAGE

Think about where your favorite products come from. Maybe they are made in a factory. Perhaps they are put together in a country far away. Somewhere, they are placed in a package. Once your favorite products are all packaged, they still need to be shipped to stores. They may be shipped around the state, country, or even around the world! They must be carefully packed in shipping boxes.

Trucks, trains, boats, and planes carry packages all around the world. Many of the packages are stored in large warehouses before being shipped to stores or other businesses.

Shipping boxes are a very common way to send all sorts of products to where they need to be stored or sold. A shipping box is really just a rectangular prism or a cube. Though similarly shaped, shipping boxes can come in a wide variety of dimensions. A shipping box may include only one product, or it may include hundreds of them. It all depends on the size of the box and the size of its **contents**.

ON DISPLAY

After shipping boxes arrive at stores, the products go on display. Store owners use all different kinds of shelves, racks, and display cases to help show off the products they are selling. Stores of all sizes must decide the best way to organize their **inventory** (IN-vuhn-tohr-ee).

It is important to deal with size restrictions first. Organizing items to fit in the available space can sometimes be a challenge. Not only does everything have to fit, but customers need to be able to see all the items and reach them easily.

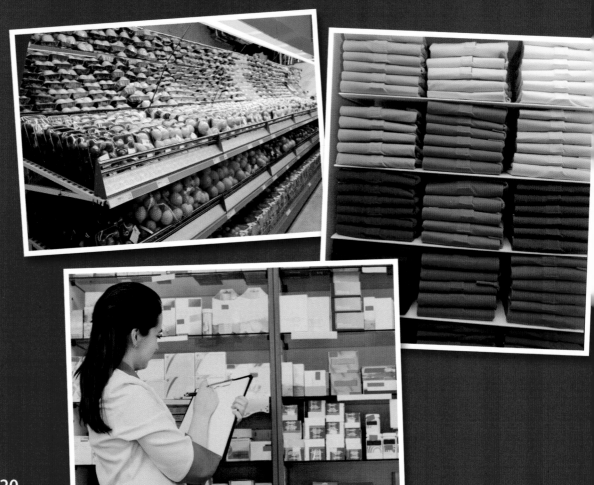

Sorting items is a smart thing to do, too. Small items might need to go up front to be seen easily. Then larger items can go on the back of a shelf. Likewise, similar types of items should be displayed together. If you were shopping in a store that sold both music and video games, it would not make sense to have these two different types of products mixed together in a display area.

LET'S EXPLORE MATH

In a grocery store, many fruits are displayed in rows of large bins. Sometimes featured fruits are put in smaller bins at the end of an aisle to catch the attention of shoppers.

One row of large rectangular bins is 6.3 feet long, 3.7 feet wide, and 2.4 feet deep. The smaller bins placed on stands next to the aisles measure 2.4 feet by 1 foot by 1.8 feet.

a. What are the volumes of these two different spaces? Round your answers to the nearest hundredth.

b. About how many loads of fruit from a small bin would fit into one row of large bins in the store?

STRATEGIC PLACEMENT

Where packages are displayed within a store is very important. Items on a store shelf are usually not placed just anywhere. There can be quite a lot of thought and planning that goes into how and where to put the packaged products.

Store owners need to think carefully about what items they want to place in the front section of the store. They may even choose to have a window display. These featured products are chosen because they will make customers want to come in and look around.

Did You Know?

Many grocery stores place certain kid-friendly products right at eye-level for a young shopper. They are hoping that a young boy or girl will see the cereal, toy, or game and beg Mom or Dad to buy it. Pretty smart placement!

Find the volume and surface area of the box below. Round to the nearest hundredth.

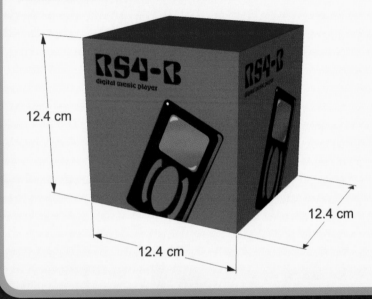

12.4 cm

12.4 cm

12.4 cm

Placing similar products on display together makes sense. But related items should be grouped together, too. For example, hair gel and hair spray should be displayed in the same area of the store because they are both hair products. Other hair products that a shopper might be interested in, like combs or hair bands, should be placed nearby.

A SAVVY SHOPPER

All companies are serious about the packaging of products. Consumers should also be serious about making smart decisions while shopping. Being a **savvy** (SAV-ee) shopper means more than finding the best price. It means making well-informed choices when you are shopping. Understanding the huge role that packaging plays in advertising can help with that. A savvy shopper knows that a company is always going to choose packaging that will help sell the product. Pay attention to the package, but also think hard about whether the product is right for you.

Paying close attention to packaging makes you a smart shopper for another reason. Packaging may provide important information about the product inside. Package labels help a shopper know more about the contents of the product. Warning labels let consumers know whether a product is appropriate for them.

Batteries power many of our favorite products. A battery closely resembles a cylinder. Find the surface area of the cylinder below.

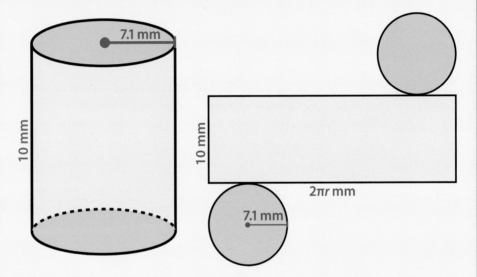

Find the area of the two circles and the rectangle, then add them together. Use 3.14 for the value of π.

a. Find the area of the rectangle. Notice that the length of the curved surface is equal to the **circumference** of the circle, $2\pi r$ or πd, where r is the radius of the circle and d is the **diameter**.

b. Find the area of one of the circles. (Remember that the area of a circle is found using the formula $A = \pi r^2$.) Double that area to include both circles. Round your answer to the nearest hundredth.

c. Find the sum of the areas of the faces. Label your answer in square millimeters (mm^2).

d. Use your work to write a formula for the surface area of a cylinder.

PACKAGED TO SELL!

From the moment a company has a new idea for a product, its advertising department is already beginning to think about how to package it. Who will buy it? What is the product used for? What do other similar products look like? All of these things and more are carefully considered. Then the product is made and packaged, boxed and shipped, and finally unloaded and put on display in your local store.

You are the most important part of this process, however. You, the consumer, are the person who makes decisions about what to buy. That means that you have a lot of power. When you look at two packages and choose one over the other, you send a powerful message to the manufacturers of both products.

What is the one thing that a company could put on a package that would help it sell? What type of packaging would make all shoppers rush to buy the product inside? That is the million-dollar question! Every company selling a product wants to know the magic ingredient for success. What do you think that might be? Until companies know the answer, they will do their best to try to make their package stand out from the crowd.

Comparing Containers

Kayla is moving into a new home. She wants to choose a container to use to move a few of her personal items. She is comparing the dimensions of three containers.

- Container A is a rectangular prism. It is 5.3 feet long and 3.1 feet wide. It has a volume of 36.17 ft.^{3}

- Container B is a cube. It measures 4.4 feet on each side.

- Container C is a cylinder. Its height is 4.75 feet. It has a radius of 1.08 feet.

Solve It!

a. Container B is a cube. What does that mean about the length, width, and height of the container? Find the volume of Container B. Round your answer to the nearest hundredth.

b. Find the volume of Container C in cubic feet. Round your answer to the nearest tenth.

c. Find the surface areas of each container in square feet.

d. If Kayla needs to know which container will take up the least amount of room in the moving truck, which measurement is most important? Why?

Use the steps below to help you solve the problems.

Step 1: Use the formula for the volume of a cube, $V = lwh$, to solve problem **a**.

Step 2: Use the formula for the volume of a cylinder, $V = \pi r^2 h$, to solve problem **b**. Use 3.14 for the value of π.

Step 3: Use the formulas for surface area to solve problem **c**.

- Surface area of a rectangular prism: $SA = 2lw + 2hw + 2lh$

- Surface area of a cube: $SA = 6s^2$

- Surface area of a cylinder: $SA = 2\pi r^2 + 2\pi rh$

advertising—the promotion of products or services in radio, television, and newspapers

area—the amount of surface enclosed by a figure

bulk—a large quantity

circumference—the perimeter of a circle

competitors—opponents that someone competes against

consumers—people who buy goods or services

contaminated—made impure or dangerous by mixing with something harmful

contents—everything that is inside a container

criterion—an accepted standard used in making decisions

cube—a solid three-dimensional figure with six congruent square faces

cylindrical—shaped like a cylinder, with two parallel and congruent regions (usually circles) joined by a curved surface

diameter—a line segment that goes through the center and connects two points on a circle

formula—a general mathematical equation or rule

inventory—the merchandise or stock that a store has on hand

net—a two-dimensional figure that can be folded to form a solid

over-the-counter drugs—medicines that can be sold without a prescription

radius—a line segment extending from the center of a circle to any point on the circle

rectangular prisms—three-dimensional objects that have six faces that are rectangles

savvy—well-informed and using good judgment

square units—units used to measure area

surface area—the total area of the faces of a solid figure

tamper-resistant—difficult to change or damage

three-dimensional—having the three dimensions: length, width, and height

two-dimensional—having the two dimensions: length and width

volume—the amount of space occupied by a three-dimensional object

ANSWER KEY

Let's Explore Math

Page 7:

a. You can find the number of cubes in the top layer by multiplying the length by the width.

b. 10 layers

c. 160 cubes

d. $V = lwh$ is the formula for volume because volume is determined by the area of the base (lw) times the height (h).

e. 3,525.08 cm^3

Page 9:

5 ft.

Page 11:

a. 120 in.^{3}

b. 28.26 in.^{2}

c. 226.08 in.^{3}

d. Soup B

e. The formula for finding the volume of the two soup containers is different because the formula for the volume of a rectangular prism is different from the formula for the volume of a cylinder.

Page 13:

a. To find the surface area, find the sum of the areas of all of its faces.

b. 9 ft.^{2}

c. 54 ft.^{2}

Page 15:

a. 30 ft.^{2}

b. 18 ft.^{2}

c. 30 ft.^{2}

d. 78 ft.^{2}

e. $SA = 2(lw) + 2(hw) + 2(lh)$ or
$SA = 2lw + 2hw + 2lh$ or
$SA = 2(lw + hw + lh)$

Page 21:

a. row of large bins: 55.94 ft.^{3}; small bin: 4.32 ft.^{3}

b. About 13 or 14 loads

Page 23:

$V = 1,906.62$ cm^3; $SA = 922.56$ cm^2

Page 25:

a. 445.88 mm^2

b. 158.29 mm^2; 316.58 mm^2

c. 762.46 mm^2

d. $SA = 2\pi r^2 + 2\pi rh$

Problem-Solving Activity

a. All dimensions of Container B are the same. $V = 85.18$ ft.^{3}

b. $V = 17.4$ ft.^{3}

c. Container A: 69.82 ft.^{2}; Container B: 116.16 ft.^{2}; Container C: 39.54 ft.^{2}

d. Volume is the most important measurement because it indicates how much space a 3-D shape occupies.